Praise for
College Essay Journal

"Among so many books and guides on applying to college, the *College Essay Journal* is an engaging and empowering workbook that truly stands out. Corinne Smith and Ann Merrell have gifted students from every background the tools needed to develop a genuine college application that students will *want* to write, and admissions officers will *want* to read."

—Jeremiah Quinlan, Dean of Undergraduate
Admissions and Financial Aid, Yale University

"Open the *College Essay Journal* and breathe a sigh of relief as Corinne Smith and Ann Merrell calmly and confidently shepherd you through one of the most daunting portions of the college application journey. Their structured, digestible, and thoughtful guide will help anyone unearth insights for their college essay and beyond."

—Allison Jegla, co-author, *Becoming Great Universities*;
former Senior Vice President, Joyce Ivy Foundation

"In the *College Essay Journal*, Corinne Smith and Ann Merrell have created a truly invaluable resource for any student embarking on the college application process. This book is packed with a plethora of accessible tips and fun writing prompts—each offering inspiration and encouraging reflection—to help students craft authentic essays that they can be proud of. How I wish I had this book when I was applying to college!"

—Matthew Akre, former undergraduate admissions and
financial aid officer, Yale University and Harvard University

"High school seniors need the *College Essay Journal*. Corinne and Ann humanize the college application process, while encouraging authenticity and individuality through short prompts. This journal would bring peace of mind to any student applying to college and reinforces that your identity, your experience, and your passions are enough."

—Lakisha Gonsalves, Learning Experience Manager,
Pursuit; former Manager of the Advising Fellowship
Experience and Impact, Matriculate

"The *College Essay Journal* focuses specifically on the student(s), not the colleges and universities. It helps flip the script of the college admissions process and brings it back to the idea that admissions is all about the student—because it is! The Mindful Manual™ helps demystify the college admissions process and go beyond high school classes, extracurriculars, and accomplishments to create a space for students to extract their authentic self and get to the meat of what all colleges want to learn about. Corinne and Ann allow for students to put practice into action through engaging activities, example prompts, and reflective activities that are useful for students in all steps of the college admissions process!"

—Rebecca Kahn-Witman, Associate Director of Admissions,
The University of Chicago Booth School of Business; former
undergraduate admissions officer, The University of Chicago

"An accessible guide like this not only supports students but demystifies the personal statement for college applicants. Corinne and Ann have outlined a practical framework that will assist educators working with students from a multitude of backgrounds and experiences."

—Pedro Ramírez, Associate Director for
Outreach and Access, Colorado College

"Corinne Smith and Ann Merrell mindfully walk us down the sometimes daunting and perilous road of college application writing. This thoughtful step-by-step guide gets to the heart of what every admissions representative across the country wants in an essay—an authentic and honest opportunity to get to know the applicant. Over the course of 30 days, users of the *College Essay Journal* will undoubtedly write a killer essay, while learning and loving themselves more along the way."

—Davion Fleming, Director of Admissions, Lick-Wilmerding High School; former undergraduate admissions officer, Northwestern University

"As a mindfulness and behavioral therapist who works primarily with high school students, I am always looking for an effective and thoughtful way to help my teens navigate the stressful process of applying to college. Corinne and Ann have created a game-changing journal. This Mindful Manual™ is a *must-do* for every high school junior in America!"

—Sydnie Dobkin, LCPC; Director of Adolescent Services, Great Lakes Therapy Center; former staff therapist, The Family Institute at Northwestern University

"Who isn't stressed about college admissions these days? From students, to parents, to teachers and counselors, the pressure of college admissions is higher than ever. This Mindful Manual™ helps ease anxiety by encouraging students to patiently engage and mindfully reflect on their goals, their growth, and their future. Whether you are a student who is just beginning to think about college or you've started your college essays already, the *College Essay Journal* will help you put your best self forward."

—Eduard Ciobanu, Associate Director of College Counseling, Phillips Academy; former undergraduate admissions officer, Yale University and Williams College

COLLEGE ESSAY JOURNAL

A MINDFUL MANUAL™
FOR COLLEGE APPLICATIONS

CORINNE SMITH & ANN MERRELL

RIVER GROVE
BOOKS

The *College Essay Journal* is designed to assist readers with their college application process, by providing accurate and authoritative information in regard to the subject matter covered. It is sold with the understanding that the publisher and authors are not engaged in rendering legal, accounting, or other professional services. Nothing herein shall create an attorney-client relationship, and nothing herein shall constitute legal advice or a solicitation to offer legal advice. If legal advice or other expert assistance is required, the services of a competent professional should be sought. Because every applicant and every educational institution is unique, neither the *College Essay Journal* nor its authors or publishers make any representation, warranty or guaranty as to the success or outcome of any reader's application(s) for admission to any educational institutions.

Published by River Grove Books
Austin, TX
www.rivergrovebooks.com

Distributed by River Grove Books

Design and composition by Greenleaf Book Group and Kim Lance
Cover design by Greenleaf Book Group and Kim Lance
Art and illustrations by Corinne Smith

Publisher's Cataloging-in-Publication data is available.

Print ISBN: 978-1-63299-457-8

eBook ISBN: 978-1-63299-458-5

First Edition

To Grandma Sandy, the original college advisor
in the family. You are my inspiration for all I do.
Grandpa Ed is smiling at this one.

In memory of Dionne, a supportive friend, an
enthusiastic educator, and a dedicated advocate
for college access.

Disclaimer

All art and illustrations in the *College Essay Journal* are intended to inspire creativity. They are not meant to represent any individual person or people of any specific race, ethnicity, gender, sexual orientation, body size or shape, disability, socioeconomic status, or other demographic.

The authors of this book strongly support and advocate for diversity, equity, and inclusion in college access and the world.

Contents

WELCOME TO THE COLLEGE ESSAY JOURNAL!

Introduction

Congratulations on applying to college! This is a big accomplishment and an exciting milestone. You should be proud of all you've done and all you're about to begin. As you think about your future and what comes next, remember that the *College Essay Journal* is there to support you. The more engaged, honest, and open you are over the next 30 days, the better prepared you'll feel on this journey. Your future self will thank you for putting your time and effort into this Mindful Manual™.

NOW LET'S GET STARTED!

When thinking about applying to college, you might be feeling . . .

* Excited, happy, or eager

* Anxious, stressed, or worried

* Confused, frustrated, or overwhelmed

* Uncertain, hesitant, or disinterested

* A mix of all the above!

A lot goes into applying to college: creating a list of schools, filling out applications, writing your essay, and even applying for financial aid. It makes sense that you might feel both excited and overwhelmed at the same time. That's what the *College Essay Journal* is here to help with.

The first part of the college application process is figuring out where you want to apply. There are many schools to choose from, and narrowing down your choices can take a while. The *College Essay Journal* will help identify what matters most for your future college experience. However, it will be up to you to build a final list of schools that reflects your priorities and preferences.

Once you've narrowed down your college choices, you'll start filling out the actual applications. Sometimes it can feel as if every school's application wants different information and asks a whole new set of questions. Determining what they're looking for can be difficult. Additionally, you may have heard from teachers, counselors, and classmates that you're going to have to write an essay. In many cases, more than one!

Don't let all of this scare you. The *College Essay Journal* will help gather application content and brainstorm essay topics that are right for you.

For many applicants, figuring out what to write tends to be more challenging than filling out the applications and crafting the essays. With that in mind, you may have heard or been told "you have to be unique to get into your favorite schools." However, the reality is this: very few people end up writing a "unique" essay. This should not be your goal.

WHILE IT MIGHT NOT BE GROUNDBREAKING, ALL APPLICANTS HAVE AN INTERESTING AND AUTHENTIC STORY TO TELL.

Your task is to figure out what that story is for you. It's the job of the *College Essay Journal* to help build a narrative through your personal statement, school specific (supplemental) responses, and any other application content you might encounter.

Now, you might be wondering...

* Where do I start?
* How do I decide what to write about?
* What are admissions officers looking for?

THAT'S WHERE THE COLLEGE ESSAY JOURNAL COMES IN!

Over the next 30 days you will share aspects of your identity, values, and goals by answering guided questions. The end result is intended to be the foundation for thoughtful and honest applications filled with genu-

ine essays that capture who you are as an individual. The purpose of the journal is to brainstorm and prepare for the many different application questions that come your way. After you finish, you'll have a book full of ideas and content ready to use.

Ultimately, the *College Essay Journal* is a Mindful Manual™ for college applications. It draws out your voice, strengths, and personal qualities in a reflective way. Completing the journal will help you do the brainstorming necessary to produce a thoughtful, personal, and compelling story.

Other questions you may have...

* Do I need to be good at journaling?

* What if I've never journaled before?

* What if writing isn't my expertise?

Some people have journaled for years. For others, this is a new experience. Don't worry! The *College Essay Journal* uses fun questions, prompts, and activities to guide you. No prior knowledge is necessary to complete the manual.

What is Mindfulness?

Mindfulness means being fully present in your mind, body, and feelings. To be mindful is to be aware in the moment without adding judgment or interpretations to reality.

The *College Essay Journal* will ask you a series of daily questions that encourage you to focus on the present moment. You'll notice a strong correlation between the prompts in this journal and the questions asked on college applications.

This approach slows down the process to allow for true reflection and deep thinking. The hope is that you will also feel less stressed and more confident throughout this journey.

At the end of the 30 days, you'll have an entire journal's worth of content to use when writing your essays and completing a full college application.

How do I start?

Great question! Plan to set aside about 15 to 20 minutes each day over the course of 30 days to complete the journal. Working in a quiet space where you're able to focus is highly recommended. You'll encounter and engage with new themes in every chapter, which will make each one feel quite manageable.

You can **go to Day 0** to start practicing now.

Anything else I should know?

NOPE!
YOU'VE GOT THIS!
LET'S GET STARTED.

DAY 0
Examples

Trust the process.
All the answers are within you!

GOALS

GET COMFORTABLE WITH JOURNALING;
COMPLETE SOME SAMPLE QUESTIONS;
START WRITING!

You can do this journal at your own pace. Generally, it works best if you spend 15-20 minutes per day over 30 days.

Thoughts on journaling

* There are no good or bad reflections or ideas

* Right or wrong answers do not exist

* Don't think too hard

* Make this space your own (write in the margins, doodle, sketch, etc.)

HAVE FUN!

This process only works if you're honest, open, and vulnerable!

What are your
favorite hobbies?

drawing

baking

sports

YOU TRY IT!

You can only bring 3 items to college ... what are they?

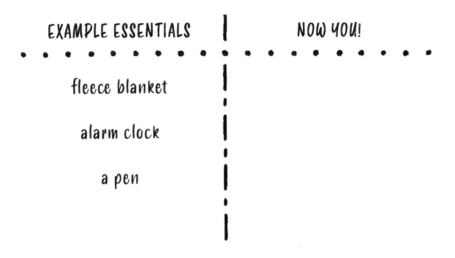

EXAMPLE ESSENTIALS	NOW YOU!
fleece blanket	
alarm clock	
a pen	

What always makes you laugh?

EXAMPLE

when animals & babies make funny faces

YOU

Describe or sketch your perfect day

EXAMPLE

going hiking in the mountains on a nice warm afternoon!

YOU

MINDFULNESS MOMENT:

What excites you about this process?

DAY 1

Beginning

Always start
at the beginning

GOALS

SET INTENTIONS FOR
THIS PROCESS; BEGIN THINKING
ABOUT WHO YOU ARE AND WHAT
YOU HAVE TO OFFER

How do you feel about applying to college?

Circle at least one

tell me more!

You'll be asked "how do you feel" throughout the *College Essay Journal*. The goal is to promote thoughtful, honest, and mindful reflection about what you're experiencing in the moment. There's no right or wrong answer!

What do you hope to gain from this? (besides a college essay)

GETTING TO KNOW YOU!

Full name: _____

Age: _____

Year in school:_____

High school: _____

Birthplace: _____

Languages spoken: _____

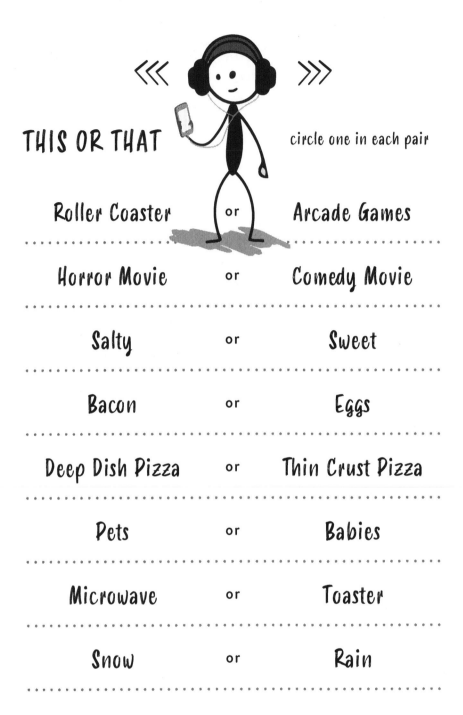

THIS OR THAT

circle one in each pair

Roller Coaster   or   Arcade Games

Horror Movie   or   Comedy Movie

Salty   or   Sweet

Bacon   or   Eggs

Deep Dish Pizza   or   Thin Crust Pizza

Pets   or   Babies

Microwave   or   Toaster

Snow   or   Rain

Why are you thinking about applying to college?

MINDFULNESS MOMENT:

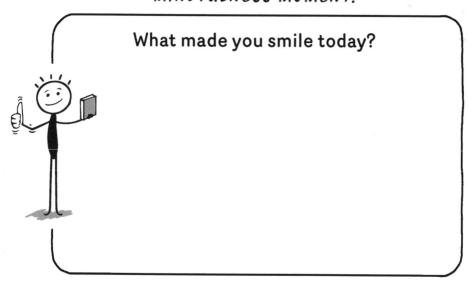

What made you smile today?

Building College Connections

* Congratulations! You've officially made it through Day 1.

* Every college's goal is to get to know you. Good thing you've just provided a number of key demographic pieces that they'll ask for up front (name, age, high school, birthplace, etc.).

* This basic information is one of the first things an admissions officer will learn about you. While it seems simple, it sets the tone for what's to come.

* If you ever feel doubtful about this process, think about why you are applying in the first place. Writing your essays can feel daunting at times, so it's important to always keep your goals and motivation at the forefront.

* Start off strong with a great first impression, and remember that you have a lot to offer!

Making It Concrete

Take your time and check your work

* Though you might complete the demographic section quickly, you'll want to make sure it is error-free and consistent across your application materials.

* Spelling, grammar, and other errors may seem small, but they can impact a school's ability to attach the correct materials to your file. You don't want anything getting lost.

Decide how schools should contact you

* If you don't already have one, create an email address that uses some combination of your first and last name. This should be the email you use on your applications and that you will check consistently throughout the process.

* Determine which phone number will go on your applications, and make sure that number has a professional-sounding voicemail message. Sometimes schools will call for interviews, with questions, or even to deliver good news.

DAY 2
Identity

No one can tell your story
the way you can

GOALS

REFLECT ON YOUR PERSONALITY
TRAITS AND CHARACTERISTICS;
THINK ABOUT WHAT PARTS
OF YOUR IDENTITY DEFINE YOU

CHECK OUT THIS IDENTITY WHEEL

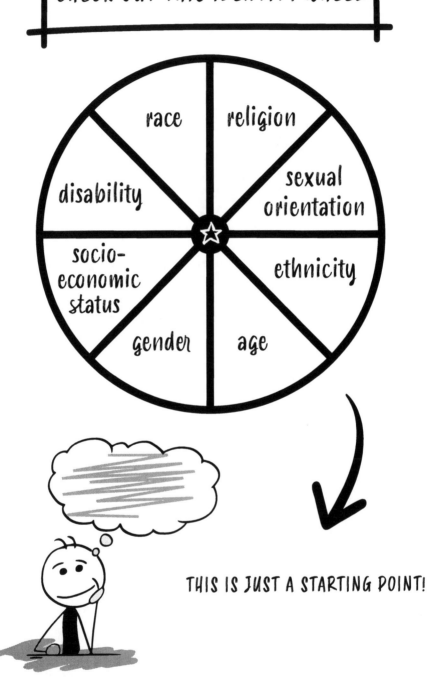

THIS IS JUST A STARTING POINT!

Fill in the bubbles with some words that make up your identity

(it's okay if you don't use them all)

Which word do you most connect with?

_____

Ask someone you trust:

"How would you describe me?"

What did they say?

How does this connect with the words you chose?

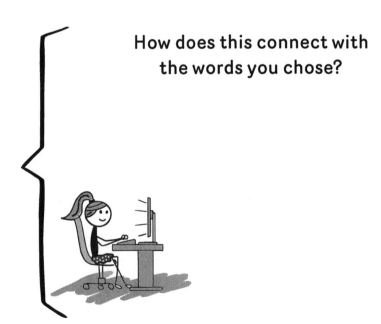

Which three songs are the current soundtrack to your life?

Put everything else away and play those songs

MINDFULNESS MOMENT:

Identify and describe something you love to do

Building College Connections

* Your identity is the foundation for your college application. It is made up of many different categories, and **you** get to decide what is important.

* Throughout this process, choose aspects of your identity that you feel comfortable sharing.

* Many great essays will address one or more aspects of the student's identity. This can be the central focus of the essay or something that is integrated into a larger story being told.

* If you don't know where to start, think about some traits that are central to who you are. These might also help you identify schools that will be a good fit.

* Remember: every piece of your file will be reviewed within the context of your specific background and opportunities.

  → For example, if an extracurricular activity is not offered in your school or neighborhood, that's okay! Admissions officers will not expect to see it on your application. They're looking to see if you maximized the experiences that were accessible to you.

  → This is also the case with the courses and curriculum offered within your high school. If certain programs or opportunities aren't available to you, don't worry.

Making It Concrete

Including identity in the college essay

1. Choose an aspect of your identity that will be the essay's **theme.**

2. Write 1 to 2 sentences to serve as the main **takeaway**.

3. Brainstorm three **topics**, ideas, or examples that will make up the body of the essay.

   → Make sure one of these connects to where you might be headed in college and beyond.

Sample Storyline:

* **Theme**: identity as a first-generation college student

* **Takeaway**: Amara will be the first in her family to attend a four-year college. This context has shaped her goals, perspective, and educational journey.

* **Topics**:

   → Growing up, Amara's parents emphasized the importance of seeking out educational opportunities and putting forth her best effort in school. They were always supportive of her academic endeavors.

   → During high school, Amara began volunteering with a mentorship group where she tutored younger students.

   → In the future, she aspires to use her college education to enter the teaching field and support other first-generation students.

DAY 3

Home

A home is more than
just a place

GOALS

UNDERSTAND HOW YOUR
ENVIRONMENT HAS SHAPED YOU;
THINK ABOUT WHAT "HOME"
MEANS TO YOU

Describe or sketch your hometown(s)

tell me more!

Have you ever moved?
{Circle one}

yes   *no*

YOUR HOMETOWN

What do you like?	What would you change?

How do you feel about
leaving home for college?

What makes a place feel like a home?

MINDFULNESS MOMENT:

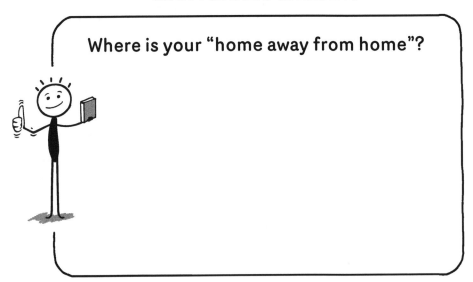

Where is your "home away from home"?

Building College Connections

* In order to decide where you want to go, it's helpful to reflect on where you come from.

* College applications will ask for information about your home as a physical place (hometown, address, who you live with, etc.). But keep in mind, a home is more than just an address.

* Your home can shape how you view the world and the values that matter on your college journey.

* Some of your most influential memories may have occurred in the place(s) you call home. These can be a great backdrop for personal statement stories and short-answer responses.

* Thinking about your home is a great way to set the scene and provide insight into your background, context, and identity.

Making It Concrete

Identify three must-haves in your future college "home" to use in your search.

✳ These can be related to:

→ School size or location

→ Architecture and green spaces

→ Gathering locations (cultural houses, office for international students, places of worship, athletic facilities, tutoring center, etc.)

→ Residential life (dorms, halls, residential colleges, small apartments, themed housing, off-campus options)

→ Or anything else that matters to you!

Sample Search:

* Luca grew up in a small town in Illinois where everyone knew each other.

* This environment shaped his idea of community and what he is looking for in a future college home.

* As he thinks about heading to college, Luca knows his three must-haves include:

    1. Being within an eight-hour drive from his family

    2. Having access to a larger metropolitan area

    3. Attending an institution with strong school spirit

* In his search, Luca filters for schools with a suburban or urban location in the Midwest with well-attended athletic events.

DAY 4

Family

You can love someone but
not always like them

GOALS

GATHER DEMOGRAPHIC INFORMATION;
REFLECT ON FAMILIAL RELATIONSHIPS;
UNDERSTAND THE INFLUENCE YOUR
UPBRINGING HAD ON YOU

GETTING TO KNOW YOU

Who do you live with?

Do you have any siblings?

If yes, what are their names? How old are they?

Did your parent(s) or guardian(s) go to college?

If yes, where?

What do your family members do for work?

How does your family feel about your college search process?

The word "family" can mean different things to different people. Feel free to use the definition that makes the most sense for you and your individual situation.

Describe or sketch your family

Share one way you are different from your family members

What are three things that bring you joy?

Ask a family member:

"What is your favorite memory with me?"

What did they say?

How do you feel today?

Circle at least one

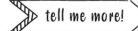
tell me more!

Building College Connections

* Similar to the demographic information you were asked to provide in Day 1, this family content will also be used in any application you complete.

* Admissions officers can learn a lot from your family background and context. It gives them insight into your identity and the opportunities available to you.

* Everyone has unique family relationships and situations.

  → For some applicants, questions about family may be straightforward, and you will already know all the answers.

  → For others, this section could be a bit more challenging. It may require having some new or uncharted conversations with people in your life. That's okay! The good news is the required family information is pretty standard across application platforms, so you should only need to gather this information once.

* Remember: these questions aren't intended to make you feel uncomfortable. Nor are admissions officers passing judgment on your family situation. All questions are asked in the spirit of understanding where you come from.

Making It Concrete

Check for accuracy

* Even if you think you know the answers, you'll want to quickly double-check. Family members' jobs and employment situations can change, and educational history may be more complex than you think.

* Ask your family members or guardians to review what you have written.

Stay mindful!

* Filling out your college applications might bring up a range of emotions. Take some time for self-care and build in breaks if you need to.

* Some mindfulness techniques include going for a walk, listening to your favorite song, doing breathing exercises, and confiding in a close friend.

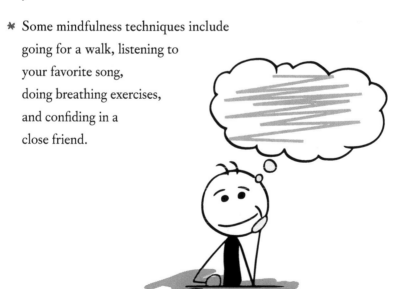

DAY 5

Friends

Trust the actions others
show you

GOALS

IDENTIFY IMPORTANT AND
SUPPORTIVE FRIENDSHIPS
IN YOUR LIFE; CONSIDER HOW
OTHERS PERCEIVE YOU

THOUGHTS ON FRIENDSHIP

Some people may have friends from childhood who will be their friends for life.

Both are great!

Other people may meet their best friends later in life.

quantity of friends ≠ quality of friends

Describe your friend group:

FILL IN THE BUBBLES WITH SOME TRAITS OR QUALITIES YOU LOOK FOR IN A FRIEND

(it's okay if you don't use them all)

Which do you value most?

What does friendship mean to you?

Ask a friend:

"What is your favorite thing we do together?"

What did they say?

MINDFULNESS MOMENT:

Share something you are grateful for

Building College Connections

* Support systems come in many shapes and sizes. For some, this might look like a large group of friends. For others, their closest confidantes may be siblings, cousins, or neighbors. There's no right or wrong here.

* It can be helpful to seek out a support system that respects how you like to spend your time and is a good fit with your distinct personality type.

  → Introverts tend to recharge on their own and may spend more time doing independent activities. Extroverts, on the other hand, are often drawn to situations with large groups or crowds. Ambiverts fall somewhere in the middle.

  → Each of these personality types is an important addition to a college's campus.

* You'll also want to think about the college setting that feels right **for you**. An institution that is a good fit will provide support and challenge you to grow while having new experiences.

* Keep in mind: the friendships you've had in the past and the role you've played in your friend group may change. Your personality can also evolve over the course of your life. Knowing that, try to enter friendships in college with an open mind and heart.

Making It Concrete

Turn the college search inward

* Identify some important relationships and support systems in your life.

* Think about your distinct personality.

* Reflect on the type of college campus that might be a good social fit.

Sample Search:

* Elena attends a large public high school where she has a close-knit group of friends. She's known a few of them since elementary school and recently expanded her social network to include some classmates on the swim team.

* While she loves going to the movies and baking with friends, Elena tends to recharge by reading books on her own. Typically, she identifies as an introvert.

* In her college search, Elena is looking for a small or medium-sized school where she can participate in intramural sports and join a book club right away.

* She filters prospective schools first by college size and then conducts additional research about the extracurricular activities available on each campus.

DAY 6

Mentors

You can respect someone
even if you disagree with them

GOALS

ACKNOWLEDGE IMPORTANT
ROLE MODELS IN YOUR LIFE;
RECOGNIZE SOURCES OF SUPPORT
AVAILABLE TO YOU

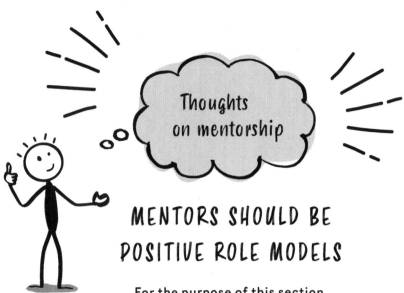

MENTORS SHOULD BE POSITIVE ROLE MODELS

For the purpose of this section,
a mentor is a person (real or fictional) who provides guidance,
motivation, and emotional support.

Who are some people you look up to?

Academically	Personally

Why do you admire these role models?

Do you feel supported in your college search?

Circle one

yes   *no*

tell me more!

Who is someone you trust to read your college essay(s) and provide honest but supportive feedback?

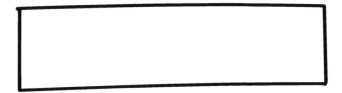

Why did you choose this person?

List 2 to 4 people who might be willing to write you a letter of recommendation

Name	Reason

-
-
-
-
-
-
-
-

MINDFULNESS MOMENT:

How can you be a role model to others?

Building College Connections

* Mentors can take on many different forms. They may be formal or informal; real or fictional; old or young. A mentor might include your favorite teacher in school, a relative who provides guidance and support, or even a character in a book that you love.

* It's important to appreciate your current mentors, but also seek out new ones upon arriving at your future college or university. A great mentor can have a significant impact on your academic success and personal growth.

* A mentor might be someone you ask to review your college application, write a letter of recommendation, conduct a mock interview, or even suggest schools that could be a good fit for you.

* Make sure to express your gratitude and appreciation for your mentor. Remember that this person is taking time out of their day to provide advice, answer questions, and invest in you. A quick "thank you" goes a long way.

* If you don't currently have a real-life mentor, that's okay! However, you may want to prioritize finding one when you arrive on campus.

Making It Concrete

Engage your mentor

* Mentors are great people to ask for helpful feedback on your college essays.

* Identify someone in your circle who fits that "mentor" role.

* Think about three questions you might ask related to the college search or essay writing process.

* When you're ready, reach out!

Conversation starters:

* What do you wish you knew when you were my age?

* What type of institution do you think I'd excel at?

* If I wasn't there and you were telling someone about me, what would you say?

* Does this college essay capture my voice and who I am?

* How might my college essay be improved?

* What advice do you have for my first semester in college and beyond?

DAY 7
Qualities

Remain open to engaging with
different viewpoints

GOALS

THINK ABOUT WHO YOU ARE
AND WHO YOU WANT TO BE;
BUILD CONFIDENCE

GIVE YOURSELF A COMPLIMENT

Share some things you are confident about and some things you'd like to improve

I've got this!	I'll work on this!

Ask someone you trust:

"What are some of my best qualities?"

What did they say? How do you feel about it?

_____

_____

_____

_____

_____

_____

_____

_____

_____

_____

_____

_____

_____

_____

_____

Describe or sketch something interesting about you

(background, context, identity, talent, etc.)

How do you feel today?

Circle at least one

tell me more!

Building College Connections

* The college search may place you at a crossroads. Part of being mindful means turning that transition into an opportunity for reflection. As you're preparing to go to college, this is a great moment to look back on who you are and decide who you want to be going forward.

* College can be an excellent place to improve or build upon the qualities you identified in this chapter. The type of institution you choose to attend will provide different opportunities for growth than you currently have.

* You'll want to engage in spaces, conversations, and activities that are currently outside of your comfort zone. You never know what skills or talents you'll discover along the way.

* When writing your college essay, take pride in the things you do well, and don't be afraid to share your strengths and accomplishments. That said, make sure you're **showing** the admissions office these traits through examples in your writing rather than just **telling** or listing them.

* Above all, engage in experiences that make you feel happy, positive, and confident in yourself.

Making It Concrete

Acknowledge your many sides

* Don't get overwhelmed if you reach a crossroads. College is all about exploration and trying new things.

* Ask yourself: what is something new you want to attempt in college?

* Identify college options that appeal to different parts of your identity.

Sample Search:

* Derrick attends a midsized independent high school in the South that is known for its football program. While he enjoys playing on the team, Derrick has started to realize he has interests in painting, drawing, graphic design, and public speaking.

* Though he wants to keep playing football, Derrick is also looking for a college with strong arts and communications departments.

* As he begins visiting schools, Derrick makes sure to ask about opportunities to take communications classes and be involved in art extracurriculars.

* Upon entering college, Derrick successfully lands a paid, on-campus job with the Athletics Department. He gets to play football on the team while also designing logos, merchandise, and social media posts.

DAY 8
List Break

LIST SOME MOVIES OR TV SHOWS YOU ENJOY

. . . .

. . . .

. . . .

. . . .

. . . .

. . . .

. . . .

☆ What about these brings you happiness?

LIST SOME OF YOUR FAVORITE BOOKS

· ·

· ·

· ·

· ·

· ·

· ·

· ·

· ·

 Is there a type of character you relate to?

How do you feel about this process?

Circle at least one

tell me more!

MINDFULNESS MOMENT:

Share something that inspires you

Finding Your Footing

* When you're ready, answer the prompt on the following page.

* This can be in the form of a full essay, a few paragraphs, or a bullet-point list. Write what comes to you!

* **Tip**: you may want to try out the "storyline format" by following the example below.

Sample Storyline:

* **Theme**: personal story focused on health and perseverance

* **Takeaway**: Cassie developed many allergies as a kid that led her to have a good sense of humor, a strong stomach, and empathy for others.

* **Topics**:

    → For three years Cassie worked at a bakery that mainly sold apple products and baked goods (think apple pie, apple donuts, apple cider, caramel apples, and apple fritters!). The food was great, but Cassie's apple allergy prevented her from eating most of it.

    → With over 40 food allergies, Cassie had to adapt and learn how to cook even though no one in her family could teach her.

    → Over time, she learned to prioritize her mind, body, and intuition while being open about these struggles.

Reflect on a piece of your identity or a
personal story that you'd like to share with
a college admissions officer.

_____

_____

_____

_____

_____

_____

_____

_____

_____

_____

_____

_____

_____

_____

_____

_____

• • •

DAY 9
Personality

Your personality is the
most interesting thing about you

GOALS

RECOGNIZE YOUR CHARACTER TRAITS; FEEL COMFORTABLE GIVING AND RECEIVING PRAISE; ACCEPT THAT THERE ISN'T JUST ONE RIGHT ANSWER

PUT A STAR ON THE SCALE FOR WHERE YOU FALL ON THESE PERSONAL TRAITS AND QUALITIES

Spontaneous	⊢————————⊣	Deliberate
Daring	⊢————————⊣	Cautious
Outgoing	⊢————————⊣	Reserved
Energetic	⊢————————⊣	Calm
Practical	⊢————————⊣	Emotional
Rigid	⊢————————⊣	Flexible
Trusting	⊢————————⊣	Skeptical
Adventurous	⊢————————⊣	Conventional
Conservative	⊢————————⊣	Liberal
Dreamer	⊢————————⊣	Realist
Creative	⊢————————⊣	Directed
Opinionated	⊢————————⊣	Open-Minded
Collaborative	⊢————————⊣	Independent
Modest	⊢————————⊣	Bold
Introverted	⊢————————⊣	Extroverted
Efficient	⊢————————⊣	Thoughtful
Determined	⊢————————⊣	Easy-Going
Silly	⊢————————⊣	Serious

Ask someone close to you:

"Which trait(s) do you most identify with me?"

What did they say?

Reflect on how your personal qualities might help
or hinder you in the future

Help	Hinder

LIST THREE TRAITS YOU WANT TO DEVELOP FURTHER

 1

 2

2 3

- -

How might attending college help you develop these traits?

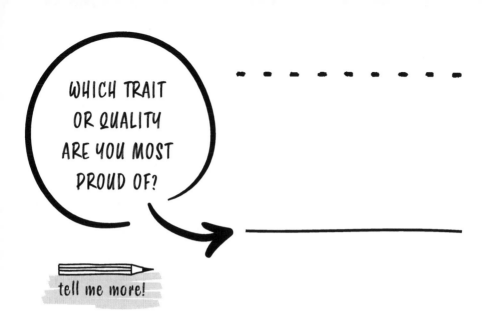

WHICH TRAIT OR QUALITY ARE YOU MOST PROUD OF?

tell me more!

- - - - - - - - - - -

_____

MINDFULNESS MOMENT:

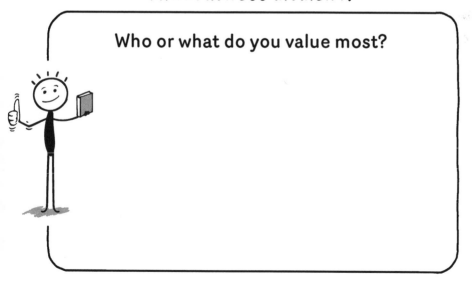

Who or what do you value most?

Building College Connections

* Your personality will likely build off the qualities listed in Day 7. It may also be heavily influenced by your family, friends, home, and other experiences.

* There are many pieces that make up your personality: are you an introvert, extrovert, or ambivert? Do you tend to be quiet or loud? Is it in your nature to listen or to speak? Would you say your strengths lie in being a leader or a follower? College campuses need all these personality types!

* These traits develop and change over time. Meaning, everyone is a work in progress. But choosing a school that's a good fit can help your personality grow and flourish.

* On some college campuses, you'll be able to dive right into a leadership role. On others, you may be asked to listen closely during small seminars or discussions. You can learn to adapt depending on the situation.

* What's important is being your authentic self. Search for a school where your personality will be valued and add to the environment.

* One of the best ways to demonstrate your personality is through your college essays. Don't be afraid to let it shine through! Schools that value you will appreciate the authenticity.

Making It Concrete

Explore online resources and social media content

* You don't have to visit a campus to get a sense of its community and culture.

* Choose your favorite social media platform or do a quick online search for videos, blogs, brochures, or brief articles in the school's newspaper. You may want to do this for at least a few schools on your college list.

* Current students and faculty are often featured in video interviews or written content. You can gain insight into campus life by checking out different online platforms.

* Ask yourself if these are the types of students and professors you'd want to interact with on a daily basis. Does it seem like they would be the kind of classmates, roommates, and teachers that would appreciate your personality? Will they help you grow during your time in college?

DAY 10

Values

Accept people for who they
are in the moment

GOALS

REFLECT ON WHAT'S
IMPORTANT TO YOU;
ACKNOWLEDGE
SOME THINGS YOU NEED
TO BE HAPPY;
SET VALUE-BASED GOALS

For the purpose of this section, values are things you believe are important to your life, studies, and relationships.

VALUES SHOULD INFLUENCE
YOUR PRIORITIES

• • •

Circle the values
that are most important to you

(aim for 3 to 5)

Authenticity	Fun	Openness
Autonomy	Growth	Optimism
Balance	Happiness	Recognition
Boldness	Honesty	Respect
Collaboration	Humor	Responsibility
Compassion	Influence	Security
Creativity	Justice	Wisdom
Determination	Kindness	
Fairness	Leadership	
Faith	Loyalty	

This is
just a starting
point!

• • •

PICK THE VALUE
MOST IMPORTANT TO YOU

Why did you choose this one?

SET THREE GOALS BASED ON YOUR VALUES

 1

 2

 3

REFLECT ON WHY THESE GOALS ARE IMPORTANT TO YOU

MINDFULNESS MOMENT:

Share some ways you stay on track

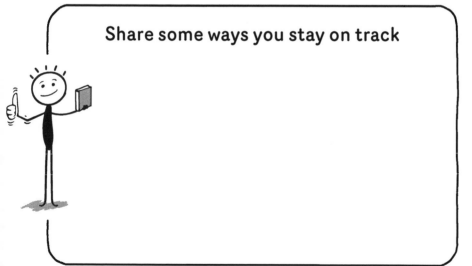

Building College Connections

* While the personality traits you identified in Day 9 are likely to be outward facing, values are often more internal.

* Your values are key to essay writing! By the end of your personal statement, the reader should be able to picture your potential contributions both inside and outside of the classroom.

* Values are important because they can inform your long-term goals, future path, and overarching direction.

* Many schools will include their values on the institution's webpage. Take a look. Do your values align with theirs? What are the similarities? What differences could be deal breakers?

* Remember: values are as unique as fingerprints. What someone else prioritizes may be different than what matters to you. Don't let a friend, family member, classmate, or anyone else determine what is important to you.

Making It Concrete

Turn the college search inward

* What three values did you identify earlier in this section?

* Think about the ways these values inform your future goals and college search.

* Reflect on the type of college campus that might be a value-based fit.

Sample Search:

* Sondra attends a large high school in a busy suburb. Over the past year she has found herself longing for more philosophical conversations, deep connections, and opportunities to explore.

* In her college search, Sondra values 1) belonging, 2) intellectualism, and 3) adventure.

* Sondra realizes she is looking for a small school with a casual and relaxed environment. She wants to be able to walk around campus and know people wherever she goes.

* It is also important for Sondra to find many opportunities for both international experiences as well as research.

* She filters prospective schools by college size, student-to-faculty ratio, and the availability of study abroad programs.

DAY 11

Community

Don't be afraid to
take up space

GOALS

UNDERSTAND YOUR ROLE
AND THE IMPACT YOU HAVE
IN THE SPACES YOU OCCUPY;
DEFINE "COMMUNITY"

For the purpose of this section, community refers to a group that shares a common belief, environment, interest, involvement, or need.

Thoughts on community

SOME PEOPLE MAY NOT FIND THEIR COMMUNITY RIGHT AWAY . . . THAT'S PERFECTLY OKAY!

What does community mean to you?

FILL IN THE BUBBLES WITH SOME SPACES OR COMMUNITIES YOU'RE A PART OF

(it's okay if you don't use them all)

★ ★ ☆ ★ ☆ ★ *
Community

Which community do you most connect with?

Ask a member of this community:

"What role do I play in this space?"

What did they say?

What do you gain from your communities, and what do you contribute to them?

Gain	Contribute
•	
•	
•	
•	
•	
•	
•	
•	
•	
•	
•	
•	

Describe or sketch a community you'd like to join or create

MINDFULNESS MOMENT:

Imagine your dream vacation or day off

Building College Connections

* A community doesn't have to be a physical space or location. It can include cultural centers, faith-based organizations, sports teams, school or neighborhood clubs, a group of friends, a volunteer program, summer camp, and many others.

* Community is also a feeling you might get when surrounded by people who share your interests, beliefs, identity, environment, or even future aspirations. If you haven't quite found the place where you "belong," college provides a wonderful opportunity to explore.

* Your participation in and dedication to a community can ebb and flow over time. You may find new communities you want to join throughout your life. It's a journey that depends on your priorities at a given moment!

* Think about what you are gaining from and contributing to any potential community. Is it a worthwhile investment?

* A great thing about college is that you can explore many new communities but also create your own if something doesn't already exist. It's easy to be the founder of an organization, join a brand-new group, or even gather informally with like-minded individuals.

Making It Concrete

Including community in the college essay

1. Choose a community that will be a part of the essay's **theme**.

2. Write 1 to 2 sentences to serve as the main **takeaway**.

3. Brainstorm three **topics**, ideas, or examples that will make up the body of the essay.

   → One of these should connect to the types of communities you would want to be a part of in college and beyond.

Sample Storyline:

* **Theme**: desire to turn a high school hobby into a college community

* **Takeaway**: Anthony has always loved history, politics, and debate. He wants to expand his knowledge of local elections and community issues by engaging in political discussions during college.

* **Topics**:

   → Throughout high school, Anthony has researched a number of global issues and current events for his role on the debate team.

   → Junior year, he took on a leadership position as the research captain who oversaw training of all new members. This sparked an interest in teaching others how to conduct research, consider multiple points of view, and engage in deep discussions.

   → In college, Anthony is interested in taking history classes and joining the Political Union. Yet, he's also started developing an idea for a student-run publication focused on political research. He's looking forward to being around others who share his enthusiasm, even if they have different viewpoints.

DAY 12

Travel

Love who you are while
on the journey

GOALS

MANIFEST IDEAS
INTO REALITY;
ASPIRE
TO EXPLORE;
ENVISION TRAVEL
POSSIBILITIES

Is traveling a big part of your life?

yes   Circle one   *no*

Who is your ideal travel companion?

Why did you choose this person?

What languages would you be
interested in learning?

LIST SOME PLACES YOU'D LIKE TO EXPLORE

Describe or sketch a physical place
that brings you joy

Reflect on your approach to exploration
or experiencing something "new"

_____

_____

_____

_____

_____

_____

_____

_____

MINDFULNESS MOMENT:

What positive thing can you do today?

Building College Connections

* College is a fantastic time to explore both on campus and around the world.

* Most schools will offer unique travel opportunities as a part of the undergraduate experience. They might have international study abroad programs, service-learning trips, class excursions to engage with course topics, summer internships, or research experiences around the country and overseas.

* College is also a place where you'll meet new people from various locations. These friendships could lead to new ways of seeing the world.

* Keep in mind that travel is not just a chance to visit a new place but to engage with other cultures, languages, histories, and ways of living.

* Whether or not you've traveled previously, try to be open to the possibility of going somewhere new. Though it's unfamiliar territory, you'll never know what you might find.

* The best part about traveling in college is that the school will typically send your financial aid with you and allow you to bring course credit back to campus.

Making It Concrete

Embrace exploration

* Travel can be exceptionally fun, but it's also a chance to embrace academic and cultural experiences.

* How might visiting a new place tie back to the things you want to learn or study?

* Identify college options that allow for exploration while meeting your academic, social, and financial needs.

Sample Search:

* Malia currently attends a public high school outside of a college town. However, due to her dad's job, Malia's family moved around the country every few years as she was growing up.

* While she has a close relationship with her immediate family, Malia has always wanted to be more engaged with her Native American heritage and community.

* Malia is open to travel and attending school far from home. Location is not a major factor in her college search.

* That said, she is focused on finding a school that offers opportunities to learn indigenous languages, supports her desire to conduct research on education, and will fund trips to visit reservations around the country.

* Malia conducts a national college search. She narrows in on research institutions with Native American Studies programs and travel grants for undergraduate students.

DAY 13

Impact

Try not to judge someone
based solely on the best or worst
thing they've done

GOALS

REFLECT ON ISSUES OF LOCAL, NATIONAL, AND INTERNATIONAL IMPORTANCE; THINK ABOUT WAYS YOU CAN MAKE AN IMPACT

FILL IN THE BUBBLES WITH SOME ISSUES YOU CARE ABOUT

(it's okay if you don't use them all)

ISSUES

Which issue do you care about most?

If you had the money or resources, how would you address this issue?

How can a college education provide you with the experiences, skills, or resources you need to approach and solve problems?

Can you make an impact in one of your communities right now?

yes   Circle one   *no*

How do you feel today?

Circle at least one

tell me more!

Building College Connections

* There are many ways to make an impact. Some examples include helping your neighbor carry their groceries, organizing a fundraiser for the local library, tutoring younger kids, writing a letter to a political official, or participating in a beach cleanup. You might just want to read the news and pay attention to what is happening in your community or hometown. All of these are great ways to start getting involved.

* Anyone can make an impact on a large or small scale. Don't focus on recognition or doing something groundbreaking. Instead, think about the ways you can make a positive difference.

* When it comes to impact, what really matters is investing your time and effort in a sincere way. Choose to engage in issues or causes that truly matter to you. These might be different from the things your friends, family, or classmates care about.

* If you haven't been involved in this way before, that's okay. You can start at any time.

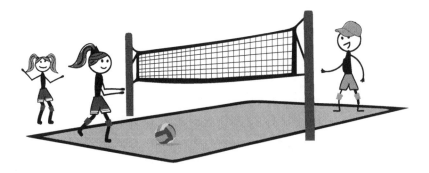

Making It Concrete

Think about how you can make an impact in school

Here are some examples:

* Participate in school-wide service days

* Volunteer at a local elementary school

* Take part in a community race

* Register local constituents to vote

* Grow produce at the campus farm

* Lead bake sales to raise awareness for a cause

* Curate an art installation to promote a message

* Coach a youth sports team

* Run a bingo fundraiser

* Play in a volunteer orchestra

* Serve as a mentor or tutor

* Join an affinity group

* Or anything else that appeals to you

Turn the college search inward

* Look at the list of activities offered at the schools you are considering.

* Do any of these stand out?

* How might you engage others in the causes you care about?

DAY 14
Activities
Part I

Go for a walk because
you like walking, not because
you're in a walking club

GOALS

DISCUSS HOW YOU SPEND YOUR TIME;
IDENTIFY ACTIVITIES THAT
HAVE MEANING TO YOU WITHIN
YOUR HIGH SCHOOL COMMUNITY

(Circle) some _in-school_ activities you have been involved with

School Government	Mock Trial	DECA/FBLA
Newspaper or Yearbook	Dance	Book Club
Band	Model UN	Language Club
Orchestra	Debate Team	Math Team
A Cappella/ Choir	National Honor Society	ROTC
Sports Teams	Speech Team	Service Club
Robotics	Cultural Club	Other: _____
Science Olympiad	Drama	Other: _____

Which three activities have been most meaningful to you?

(they don't have to be on this list)

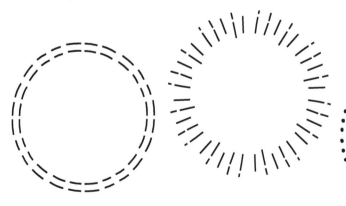

Pick your favorite <u>in-school</u> activity

Describe the activity:

What was your role?

What have you learned from it?

SHARE SOMETHING ABOUT THIS ACTIVITY
THAT GETS YOU EXCITED

Ask someone from this activity:

"What has my involvement meant to you?"

What did they say?

MINDFULNESS MOMENT:

How can you make yourself a priority today?

Building College Connections

* There are infinite activities for students to join or take part in. Some of these will take place at school, while others will occur in your everyday life. You'll dive into these out-of-school activities further on Day 15.

* Given the sheer number of extracurriculars that exist, choosing which ones to pursue can be difficult. Some students will find themselves stretched too thin. Others may not have access to the organizations that truly interest them while in high school. Make sure to check in with yourself and prioritize the activities that get you excited.

* Building on this idea, the "well-rounded" student will engage in many types of activities all at once. On the other hand, the "narrowly focused" student might find themselves diving deeply into one or two interests. Colleges need both types of students on their campus. It's all about quality over quantity!

* Remember: schools are building an entire class and have hundreds of activities that need participants. They're looking for leaders and members for all of them.

* Don't feel compelled to join a club because it's popular or your friends are in it. Carve your own path and stay open to trying new things.

Making It Concrete

Reflect on your involvement

* On your college application you'll be asked to create a list of approximately 5 to 10 extracurricular activities you have been involved in.

* The extracurricular list can include almost anything you do outside of class. It can be filled with clubs and organizations, volunteer work, athletics teams, involvement in the arts, hobbies, family responsibilities, and part-time work.

Tips for filling out your extracurricular list:

* Put your most significant or meaningful involvement first.

* Try to include more recent activities towards the top.

* Make sure to write out all acronyms.

* If you don't have enough space to briefly explain a more obscure activity, you can always use the "additional information" section of the application.

* Be honest about your time commitments and the hours you spend on each activity.

* Include any leadership positions, major contributions, or awards.

* Quantify when possible.

    → If you organized a fundraiser, how much money did you raise?

    → If you led a club, how many members did you oversee?

* Your list should not include activities from elementary or middle school.

* Generally, "activities" will involve other people.

    → Reading books for fun, playing video games,
      or going on a walk after dinner aren't exactly what
      admissions officers are looking for.

    → However, taking part in a book club, teaching others
      to code, or participating in a community trail-running
      group would be great!

* Be succinct and mindful of any word limits. You'll likely only have
  a sentence or two to explain your involvement.

DAY 15

Activities
Part II

Building a life is more important
than building a résumé

GOALS

DISCUSS HOW YOU SPEND YOUR TIME;
IDENTIFY ACTIVITIES WITH
MEANING TO YOU OUTSIDE OF
YOUR HIGH SCHOOL COMMUNITY

(Circle) some activities you have been involved with **outside of school**

Hobbies	Job Shadowing	Civic Engagement
Part-Time Job	Community-Based Organization	Theater
Internship	Watching Younger Siblings	Camp
Research	Fundraising	Academic Programs
Volunteering	Advocacy	Learning Languages
Faith-Based Group	Campaign Work	Babysitting
Taking Care of Family	Playing an Instrument	Other: _____
Tutoring	Independent Projects	Other: _____

Which three activities have been the most meaningful to you?

(they don't have to be on this list)

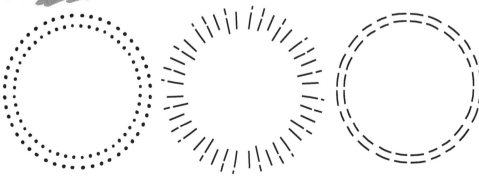

Pick your favorite <u>outside of school</u> activity!

Describe the activity:

What was your role?

What have you learned from your involvement?

{ Is there something about this activity that
makes you proud to be involved? }

Ask someone from this activity:

"What has my involvement meant to you?"

What did they say?

MINDFULNESS MOMENT:

**Think of something to do outdoors
(then go do it!)**

Building College Connections

* In Day 14 you focused on developing an extracurricular list. Today, you'll reflect on how this involvement can become a part of your college essay.

* As you do this, be aware that activities taking place outside of school can be equally important to those happening at school.

* You may have important responsibilities at home or in your community that admissions officers want to learn about. You should share these if you're comfortable.

* There is no magical extracurricular list that will guarantee acceptance to the college of your choice. In fact, it would be unfortunate if every student on a college's campus participated in the same activities during high school.

  → Imagine a campus filled with only baseball players. Who would run cross country or wrestle or play in the intramural Ultimate Frisbee league?

  → If every student wanted to be the student body president, how would that work? There would be no one to fill other student government roles and keep the organization running.

* As you fill out your application, you may want to take a look at the activities available at some of the schools on your list. College is a place where you can find activities you've never heard of (Lettuce Eating Club, the October Lovers Organization, or Medieval Knight Dinner) or try out something new that you've always been interested in (rugby, knitting, or a cappella singing to name a few).

* Just because you've done something throughout high school doesn't mean it has to be your focus in college. It's the perfect time to try new activities.

Making It Concrete

Including activities in the college essay

1. Choose an activity you are involved in that will be a part of the essay's **theme**.

   * It can be an activity in which you are a leader or a member.

2. Write 1 to 2 sentences to serve as the main **takeaway**.

3. Brainstorm three **topics,** ideas, or examples that will make up the body of the essay.

   * One of these should connect to your potential involvement in college or beyond.

Sample Storyline:

* **Theme**: building relationships and learning from elder community members

* **Takeaway**: After her grandmother passed away, Katrina started planning events for elders at a local community center. She discovered a love for helping others.

* **Topics**:

    → Katrina was very close to her grandma growing up. They spent every weekend together, and there was nothing Katrina loved more than hearing her stories.

    → She decided to carry on her grandmother's legacy through volunteer work at a local retirement community. Eventually, Katrina took on a leadership role planning monthly events such as bingo, birthday parties, and craft nights.

    → In college, Katrina hopes to connect with a local retirement community where she can continue this work, chat with the residents, and meet other volunteers. She also hopes some of her college friends will participate and enjoy giving back.

DAY 16

List Break

LIST SOME MUSIC OR PODCASTS YOU LISTEN TO

. . . .

. . . .

. . . .

. . . .

. . . .

. . . .

. . . .

. . . .

. . . .

How do these make you feel
while listening?

LIST SOME MEALS, RESTAURANTS, OR FOODS THAT YOU ENJOY

· ·

· ·

· ·

· ·

· ·

· ·

· ·

· ·

Who is your favorite person to share a meal with and why?

How do you feel about this process?

Circle at least one

tell me more!

MINDFULNESS MOMENT:

Who or what made you laugh recently?

Finding Your Footing

* When you're ready, answer the prompt on the following page.

* This can be in the form of a full essay, a few paragraphs, or a bullet-point list. Write what comes to you.

* **Tip**: you may want to use the "storyline format" from previous sections.

  → Remember: theme, takeaway, and topics!

Share an experience related to the
themes of community, activities, or travel.
Reflect on how the experience impacted
you and what you learned from it.

DAY 17

Academics

Perfection is a concept,
not a reality

GOALS

IDENTIFY YOUR ACADEMIC
PRIORITIES; DISCOVER WHO YOU
ARE IN THE CLASSROOM;
ENVISION FUTURE OPPORTUNITIES

What is your favorite class or subject?

Why did you choose this one?

○ GIVE YOURSELF A COMPLIMENT ○

Describe or sketch your favorite teacher

What qualities make this person so effective and impactful?

Complete the sentence

If I were teaching a class, it would be . . .

_____

_____

Which class do you currently enjoy the least?

Which class are you most excited for in college?

MINDFULNESS MOMENT:

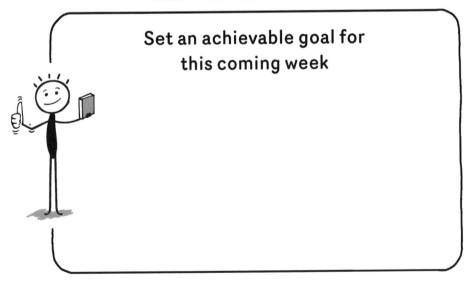

Set an achievable goal for this coming week

Building College Connections

* First and foremost, college is an academic experience. You'll want to make sure the schools on your list fit with your intellectual priorities and offer classes you are interested in taking.

* That said, most students around the country will change their major at least once during college. At some schools this number is as high as 80%! Keeping this in mind, try to stay open to exploration. There may be classes and majors you've never heard of before that will grab your attention.

* It's also okay to be completely undecided. On a college campus you will have advisors and academic support helping to identify the right major for you. You'll want to take advantage of these resources by reaching out, asking questions, and seeking advice.

* It's important to reflect on the type of learning environment that works best for **you**. Here are some questions to ask yourself:

  → Do you learn best in a small or large classroom?

  → Are you a visual, auditory, verbal, or hands-on learner?

  → How much do you value working independently versus in a group?

  → Do you picture yourself in a lab, a traditional classroom, an art studio, or some other setting?

  → What type of relationship would you like to have with your professors?

* **Tip**: try not to be overly focused on the distant future. Think about the next four years before the four after that.

Making It Concrete

Academics in action

* Reflect on your academic experiences so far.

  → What have you liked?

  → What would you change?

* Research some majors and classes you haven't had a chance to take.

* Identify college options that allow for exploration while meeting your academic goals.

Sample Search:

* Sebastian has always enjoyed his math and science classes. During senior year of high school many of his friends were taking cool history and English electives, but there weren't as many offerings in his areas of interest.

* Outside of school, Sebastian would watch videos to learn more about advanced physics. He also focused his time on becoming an Eagle Scout and played saxophone in the marching band.

* The top priority in Sebastian's college search was finding advanced classes in physics and calculus. While he had heard about engineering, his high school didn't offer any courses in this subject area.

* During a college visit, Sebastian took a tour of an engineering design center and fell in love. He realized this was the type of hands-on work he enjoyed that also incorporated math and science.

* The schools on Sebastian's final college list all had strong engineering departments but also allowed him to explore different majors.

* By the end of his second year in college, Sebastian officially declared a major in mechanical engineering, joined an engineering social organization, and started playing saxophone in a jazz band.

DAY 18

Curiosities

Intelligence and success are
not finite resources

GOALS

RECOGNIZE WHAT INSPIRES
YOU TO THINK, LEARN, AND CREATE;
DON'T HOLD YOURSELF BACK

Describe or sketch what makes you
fall down the rabbit hole

(websites, videos, social media . . .)

• • •

When your mind wanders,
where does it go?

If you had dinner together, what would you talk about?

(What would you tell them about yourself?)

You just won the Nobel Prize . . .

What was it for?

What event in history would your time machine take you to?

Give a quick recap of the book that has meant the most to you

MINDFULNESS MOMENT:

What's something fun you can do this week?
(go do it!)

Building College Connections

* In college you will be surrounded by all types of people who value learning. Students, faculty, and staff will each add to your educational journey in unique ways.

* Those around you will have different life experiences, backgrounds, and interests. Think of this as a positive! It's a great opportunity to learn from diverse individuals and engage with interests that get others excited.

* College is not just about gaining technical skills or completing a degree. It is also important to explore curiosities and engage in lifelong learning. When possible, take classes outside of your specific major or department. In life there will be countless moments when you can draw upon this knowledge.

* You'll learn just as much outside of the classroom as inside of it. Don't underestimate the importance of late-night conversations with roommates, getting to know the community around campus, and spontaneously going to events.

* Enjoy the journey, not just the destination.

Making It Concrete

Go where life takes you

* Engaging in the college search and application process may inspire you to learn something new.

* Take some time to let your mind wander and delve into these areas of interest.

* You don't have to wait until college to follow your curiosities and see where they lead you.

Stay mindful!

* Listening to a podcast, reading a book, sketching, watching educational videos, and engaging in conversations about a concept that fascinates you are all great ways to explore your curiosities.

DAY 19

Happiness

Don't let others decide
what you enjoy

GOALS

IDENTIFY WHAT BRINGS YOU JOY;
BUILD INTENTIONALITY AND
POSITIVITY; REALIZE YOU MAKE
YOUR OWN HAPPINESS

How do you feel today?

Circle at least one

tell me more!

 ## What was the last thing that made you smile?

SHARE THREE THINGS
THAT MAKE YOU
HAPPY

Who do you turn to with exciting news?

➥ _____

Does this person provide support?

yes **Circle one** ✏️ *tell me more!* no

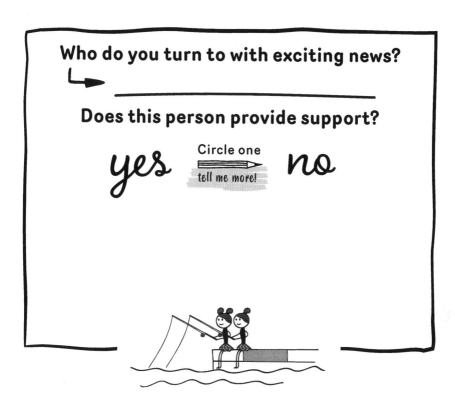

When do you get so engaged that time stands still?

Describe or sketch your vision
for a "happy future"

MINDFULNESS MOMENT:

Share a positive thought or aspiration

Building College Connections

* At some points the college search and essay writing processes may seem tedious or overwhelming. It's important to prioritize your mental health and happiness at every stage. Don't be afraid to take a break and come back later if needed.

* As you write, keep your goals and priorities in mind. Think about building a future that gets you excited.

  → Remember what you described or sketched as a part of your "happy future."

  → Seize opportunities that genuinely interest you and use those to shape your goals.

  → Find activities to keep you motivated.

* You should also include others who offer positive support in your journey. Share your happiness or joy with them as you go. These people will be excited for you regardless of where you end up attending school.

* Applying to college is a big step toward your future. Take a moment to reflect on how far you have come over the past few years. It's a huge accomplishment!

* Finally, recognize how awesome it is that you're taking the time to do the *College Essay Journal* and reflect in a mindful way. Be proud of yourself.

Making It Concrete

Share your search

* As you're learning about colleges, engage others in the process.

* Identify someone you trust who will provide honest feedback and make helpful recommendations.

* Share the things that make you happy, and don't be afraid to ask questions.

Sample Script

* **Student**: Hey! I was doing some research and found this school . . . I've never heard of it before, but it seems to check all the boxes I'm looking for. Should I apply?

* **Counselor**: Wow. That's so exciting. Do you want to share more? What makes it a good fit for you?

* **Student**: Well, it has a conservatory-style music program, but I can still major in economics and take other classes in biology. I also noticed that the campus is just a short train ride from the city where I can do an internship and check out museums with new friends on the weekends.

* **Counselor**: It sounds like you should definitely apply there! Can I help you look for some other schools that are similar? This seems like it might be your top choice, but we should make sure you have a well-rounded list of places you'd be happy at.

* **Student**: Yes, please! You are always so supportive, and it means a lot to me.

* **Counselor**: Please know that I'm here for anything you need. I'm always on your team.

DAY 20

Challenges

Two opposing things can exist and
be true at the same time

GOALS

RECOGNIZE HURDLES
OR OBSTACLES; LEARN TO
PROCESS THEM IN A POSITIVE
AND MINDFUL WAY

What was something that recently challenged you?

Share three situations or circumstances you find difficult

Who do you turn to when you're sad or facing an obstacle?

_____

Does this person provide positive support?

yes   Circle one
          tell me more!   *no*

How do you cope with failure?

Describe or sketch a time when "everything worked out"

How do you feel today?

Circle at least one

tell me more!

MINDFULNESS MOMENT:

Who is impacted when you're sad?

Building College Connections

* Day 19 centers around finding support systems who share your happiness or excitement. Today, you'll want to identify people you can turn to when things don't go as planned.

* Facing challenges is a part of life. Experiencing them does not make you weak or a failure. Every challenge is an opportunity to learn and grow. You should try to embrace obstacles and use them as motivation going forward.

* When identifying your support system, choose people who will give thoughtful advice, provide a new perspective, and help reframe challenges using a positive narrative.

* Sometimes you simply don't want to feel alone. Having someone to keep you company can be just as important as receiving guidance. Don't underestimate the value of being around someone who cares.

* For smaller setbacks, there's something to be said for laughing off a challenging situation and moving on. This applies to much more than your college essay or application outcomes!

* When you experience an obstacle, try to approach it with a positive mindset. If you are writing about this type of event for a college essay, how you reflect on the situation will be exceptionally important.

Making It Concrete

Tips for writing about "challenges" or "failures"

* **Take ownership and accountability**. Avoid assigning blame or complaining. Instead, shift to problem-solving and focus on growth.

* **Don't get stuck in the past**. It's easy to become overly focused on the negative experience. Instead, try to move to the present (or even the future) quickly.

* **Stay mindful**. When talking about challenges, keep a positive tone and mindset. Admissions officers will assess your attitude in the essays just as much as your words.

* **Resilience is an asset**. Give the reader a sense of your perseverance and how you might approach obstacles in the future.

* **Have some distance from the event**. If there's a challenge that you are currently experiencing, you may want to choose another topic. It will be hard to show lessons learned or growth if you're still in the thick of it.

* **Be a victor, not a victim!** You don't have to overcome hurdles or bring someone to tears to get accepted. You may not have a challenge to write about. That's perfectly fine. Don't fabricate or write about someone else's experience. Simply choose another essay topic that interests you.

DAY 21

Laughter

Small chuckles
can turn into deep laughter

GOALS

BRING SOME FUN TO THIS PROCESS;
REMEMBER TO LIVE IN THE MOMENT;
SURROUND YOURSELF WITH
PEOPLE WHO MAKE YOU LAUGH

SHARE THE LAST THING THAT REALLY MADE YOU LAUGH

What are some things you find funny?

Who makes you laugh the most?

_____

BRAINSTORM WAYS YOU CAN BRING JOY TO OTHERS

MINDFULNESS MOMENT:

Share something you do well

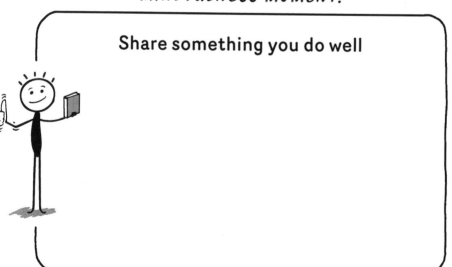

Building College Connections

* Writing your college essay is an important task. You'll want to take it seriously, but that doesn't mean every moment has to be serious.

* Don't let the writing process overtake the rest of your life. Leave room in your day for the activities you enjoy and people you care about. Prioritize spending time with others who make you laugh or doing things that bring you happiness.

* Taking time for yourself can have a positive impact on your college application.

* Admissions officers can tell if an applicant had fun with the process through their essay responses. They love when an application can make them laugh, smile, or feel like they really know the writer.

* It's okay to incorporate humor and lightheartedness into your essay responses. If you're funny, be funny. If you're not funny, don't feel like you must be funny. Above all, let your authentic personality shine through.

Making It Concrete

Find joy in the journey

* College is meant to be a fun experience both academically and socially. You'll want to take classes and join organizations that bring you joy, make you laugh, and satisfy your curiosity.

* Find a unique class or activity that might be off the beaten path and give it a try.

* Identify college options that get you excited about the next four years.

Stay mindful!

* Watching a television show you find funny, listening to a comedy special, telling your favorite embarrassing story, or playing with a pet are all great ways to find happiness and laughter.

* Remember: laughter can reduce stress, anxiety, depression, and burnout.

DAY 22

Mindfulness

Always remember to say
thank you

GOALS

INCORPORATE MINDFUL THINKING
AND PRACTICES INTO YOUR
DAILY LIFE; APPLY THEM TO
THE ESSAY WRITING PROCESS

Go outside for 20 minutes

Describe or sketch some observations

What three things make you feel calm?

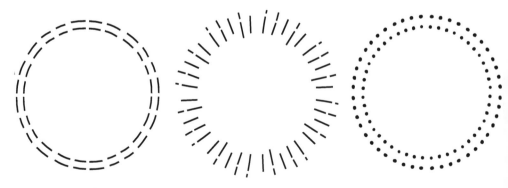

Ask someone you look up to:

"How do you cope with stress or failure?"

What did they say?

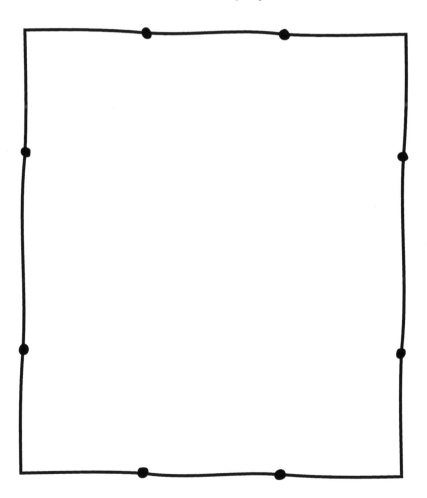

Circle some mindfulness strategies you'd like to try

Pay More Attention	Practice Meditation	Be More Intentional
Try to Slow Down	Give Yoga a Shot	Do Some Exercise
Be Aware of Your Senses	Go for a Walk	Have a Hot Drink
Live in the Moment	Try Gardening	Build a Routine
Listen to White Noise	Cook an Easy Meal	Close Your Eyes
Light a Candle	Spend Time Outdoors	Listen to Calm Music
Breathe Deeply	Sit in a Quiet Place	Laugh Out Loud
Lie on Your Back	Count Out Loud	Accept Yourself Fully

HOW CAN YOU BE KINDER TO YOURSELF?

Thoughts	Actions

- •
- •
- •
- •
- •
- •
- •
- •
- •
- •
- •

Set realistic expectations!
• • • • •

MINDFULNESS MOMENT:

How will you react to your next setback?

Building College Connections

* The *College Essay Journal* defines mindfulness as being fully present in your mind, body, and feelings. It is important to have a balance of awareness in the moment without adding judgment to a situation.

* Mindfulness can have an impact on all aspects of your life. You can use the techniques in Day 22 for everything from college essay writing to disagreements with friends to your future job search.

* There are many small ways to incorporate mindfulness into your daily routine. Try to take a few minutes each day to check in on how you feel.

* Mindfulness techniques can be used when you're happy, sad, excited, anxious, nervous, content, relieved, or feeling any other emotion. They aren't just for the overwhelming moments.

* By completing this Mindful Manual™ you've hopefully developed an amazing tool kit with many people to rely on and actions you can take when the situation calls for it.

Making It Concrete

Lessons learned from the *College Essay Journal*

* How to reflect and approach challenges with a positive mindset

* Ways to be kind and have compassion for yourself

* Coping techniques for stressful moments

* How to set realistic goals and intentions

* The importance of remaining in the present

* The need for a strong and consistent support system

* Keeping an open mind towards new or different experiences

* Appreciating the journey as well as the outcome

Turning mindfulness inward

* Picture some scenarios where practicing mindfulness could be helpful.

* What strategy will you use? Choose one to share with someone else.

* In the future, how will you incorporate mindfulness techniques into your daily life?

DAY 23
List Break

THIS OR THAT

circle one in each pair

Mountains	or	Beach
Coffee	or	Tea
Summer	or	Winter
Pancakes	or	Waffles
City	or	Country
Cats	or	Dogs
Night	or	Morning
Socks	or	Barefoot
E-book	or	Audiobook
Chocolate	or	Candy
Video Games	or	Movies
Walk	or	Bike
Sports	or	Arts
Talking	or	Listening

tell me more!

MINDFULNESS MOMENT:

Describe a time when you felt lucky

Finding Your Footing

* When you're ready, answer the prompt on the following page.

* This can be in the form of a full essay, a few paragraphs, or a bullet-point list. Write what comes to you!

* **Tip**: you may want to use the "storyline format" from previous sections (theme, takeaway, and topics).

Describe an aspect of your background, context, or personal experience that is important to you. How might this add to a college community?

_____

_____

_____

_____

_____

_____

_____

_____

_____

_____

_____

_____

_____

_____

_____

_____

_____

_____

_____

_____

[more room to keep writing]

DAY 24

Timeline

People will remember how
you make them feel

GOALS

IDENTIFY MAJOR MOMENTS IN YOUR LIFE; UNDERSTAND HOW THE PAST MIGHT IMPACT YOUR PRESENT; SET GOALS FOR THE FUTURE

Add significant moments from your life to the timeline below!

Examples: moving, parents' divorce, birth of a sibling, making the swim team!

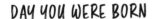

DAY YOU WERE BORN

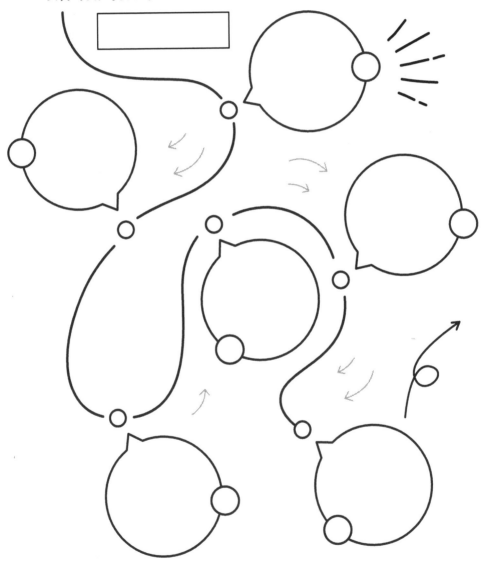

Timeline continued!

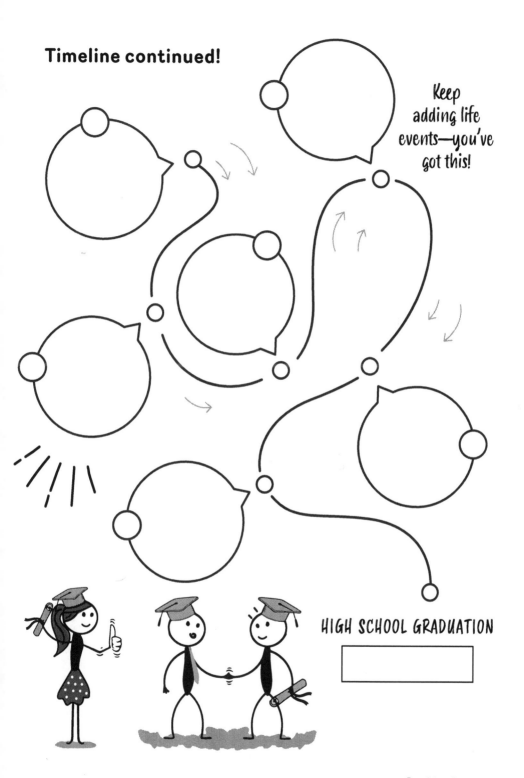

Keep adding life events—you've got this!

HIGH SCHOOL GRADUATION

What future moments are you excited about?

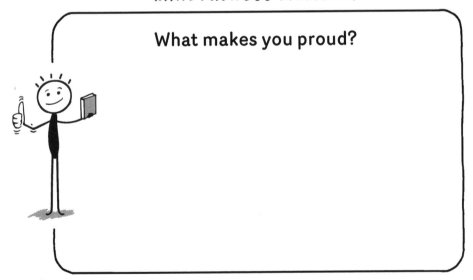

MINDFULNESS MOMENT:

What makes you proud?

Building College Connections

* Reflecting on the past can help project what you want for the future. As you look at your timeline, think about what stands out. Which events do you want your future college to know about?

* Life events are subjective. The things you consider "defining moments" don't have to be big or meaningful to anyone else. They just need to be important to you.

* Though the story is important, it should not be the full essay. Admissions officers want to read what happened, but they also care about what you learned, how you've grown, and where you are headed.

  → **Tip**: bring the essay to the present quickly. Generally, only a third (or less!) of the essay should take place in the past.

* Colleges are looking to admit the person you are now. With that in mind, reflect on the experience rather than just reciting it. Think back to the idea of "showing versus telling" from Day 7.

* Take the reader with you on the journey by setting the scene:

  → Where did it occur?

  → What did you see?

  → Who was there?

  → How did you feel?

  → When did this happen?

  → What happened afterward?

  → What did you learn?

  → Why was it important?

* The college essay is not the place to list every event from your life. It's a narrative, not a chronicle. Choose one or two main events that will serve as the backdrop for the reader to learn more about you.

Making It Concrete

Including your past in the college essay

1. Choose an experience or event that will be the backdrop for the essay's **theme**.

2. Write 1 to 2 sentences to serve as the main **takeaway**.

3. Brainstorm three **topics**, ideas, or examples that will make up the body of the essay.

   * One of these should connect to college or beyond.

Sample Storyline:

* **Theme**: turning a childhood interest into a potential career

* **Takeaway**: Suni's childhood purchase of a camera led to a lasting interest in photography. She has a strong desire to pursue this hobby in college both in and out of the classroom.

* **Topics**:

  → Suni has always liked the outdoors and exploring. While biking, hiking, and going for runs, she would often take her camera along to capture these experiences.

  → During high school, Suni took a number of photography classes. She learned the importance of lighting, how to develop her own film, and the different styles of photography.

  → In college, Suni wants to start taking professional headshots for her new college friends. She would like to work with a school's entrepreneurial center to set up a small photography business and see if this career path is the one for her.

DAY 25

Future

Who you've been is not necessarily
who you're meant to be

GOALS

REFLECT ON HOW YOU VIEW
YOURSELF; ENVISION WHO YOU
WANT TO BE GOING FORWARD

SHARE THREE POTENTIAL JOBS OR CAREERS THAT INTEREST YOU

 _____

 _____

 _____

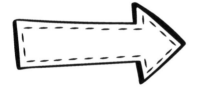 Of these three, pick
your top choice for right now

_____

Which traits make
you a good fit for this role?

Ask some friends or family members:

"What job or career could you see me in one day?"

> ### What did they say?

Did any of these jobs surprise you?

Tell me more!

HOW MIGHT COLLEGE HELP YOU TO PREPARE FOR YOUR FUTURE CAREER?

MINDFULNESS MOMENT:

What does being creative mean to you?

Building College Connections

* It is important to approach thinking about the future with an open mind. As discussed on Day 17, most students will change their major at least once during college. Similarly, adults often pursue multiple jobs throughout a lifetime.

* Mindfulness means reflecting thoughtfully about the options available to you. Appreciate each experience as it happens, and take note of the ones you enjoy.

* Experiences that don't go as planned are also meaningful learning opportunities.

* If one door closes, another will open. Try not to place your value or self-worth on a specific career or outcome. Success in life is not defined solely by your job.

* Don't let others choose your future path for you. Their strengths and interests will be different from yours.

    → Remember: you're the one who has to show up every day. What you choose to do should make **you** happy!

* See the importance of extracurriculars and networking. College students will often figure out what they want to do outside of the classroom. The light bulb moment can happen anywhere.

* The college essay and search processes do not have to focus on your future career. You can identify things you value or want to get involved in without locking yourself into one defined path.

Making It Concrete

Forecasting the future

* Consider the potential jobs, careers, or pathways that interest you.

    → Is there anything they have in common?

    → Why might you enjoy these in the long run?

* Research some majors and classes that will help you explore these future opportunities.

* Identify college options where you can pursue your goals but also try out new areas of interest.

Sample Search:

* Elliot has always loved animals and grew up rescuing frogs, turtles, hamsters, cats, dogs, and even an iguana.

* Starting in ninth grade, Elliot launched a dog-walking business with a friend, cared for pets in the neighborhood, and volunteered at the local animal shelter.

* Elliot hopes to learn more about the pathway to becoming a veterinarian and wants to attend a school that offers hands-on field experience.

* In the college search, Elliot prioritizes schools with internships or co-operative experiences, have majors in biology or zoology, and offer a pre-health track for applying to veterinary school.

* In college, Elliot continues to volunteer at a local animal hospital but decides not to pursue veterinary medicine going forward. Instead, Elliot focuses on scientific research and lab work as a future career.

DAY 26

Emotions

Emotions are involuntary;
feelings are a habit

GOALS

REFLECT ON THE WORK YOU'VE DONE;
THINK ABOUT WHAT COMES NEXT;
EMBRACE THINGS THAT ARE BOTH
SCARY AND EXCITING

How do you feel about this process?

Circle at least one

tell me more!

THINKING AHEAD TO COLLEGE . . .

Share something you're excited to experience	Is there anything that makes you a bit nervous?

What is something you expect will change next year?

What is something that will stay the same?

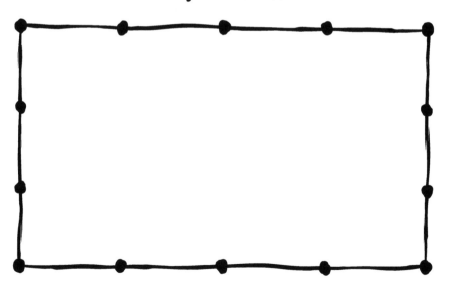

Describe or sketch how you feel about the last few questions

YOU WILL MEET MANY PEOPLE IN COLLEGE!

What do you hope to add
to their experiences?

 What do you hope they will add to yours?

MINDFULNESS MOMENT:

Share something that went well this month

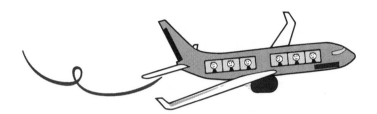

Building College Connections

* Heading off to college is a big transition no matter who you are or where you go.

* Everyone will have different emotions about this process and what comes next. It's okay if leaving for college feels both scary and exciting. It's also natural for these feelings to change from one day to another.

* You should share how you're feeling with others. Your friends, family, and mentors can't support you if they don't know what you're going through. It's a good opportunity to practice mindfulness, check in on yourself, and engage others in the application process.

* Don't avoid applying to a school because it is outside of your comfort zone. You'll have time before you make your final decision to determine if it's the right place for you. The only way to guarantee you won't get in is to not apply.

* Take the things you're excited about and try demonstrating them through your essays. What about a specific school piques your interest? Admissions officers will be looking for this type of emotional connection and enthusiasm in your writing.

* Remember: the first term in college is a transition for everyone. You're not alone if you feel nervous about fitting in or take some time adjusting to campus. Chances are those around you feel similarly.

  → **Tip**: be open with how you're feeling, and ask for help when you need it.

Making It Concrete

Coping with change

* Think about another time when you experienced a life transition.

* How did you feel? Who did you lean on for support? What coping strategies did you use?

* Be aware of college resources that can help during tough times. Some examples include:

    → College advisors

    → Counseling services

    → Health and wellness classes

    → Cultural and spiritual centers

Tips for managing complex emotions

* Take some deep breaths to relax.

* Identify the emotions you are experiencing.

* Talk to someone about how you feel.

* Spend time outdoors or in a space you find calming.

* Connect with people going through similar situations.

* Get a good night's rest.

* Write it out in a journal!

DAY 27

Finances

Important things in life can
be worth the cost

GOALS

START HAVING DISCUSSIONS
ABOUT FINANCING COLLEGE;
THINK ABOUT BUDGETING;
EXPLORE POTENTIAL CAREER PATHS

PUT A DOLLAR SIGN ON THE SCALE TO SHOW WHERE YOU FALL ON THESE BUDGET-RELATED TRAITS

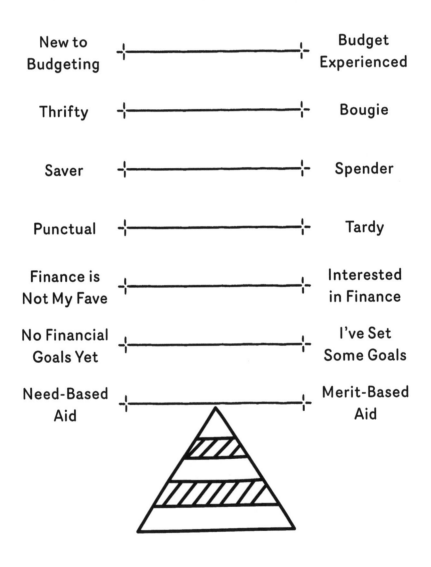

New to Budgeting ——————— Budget Experienced

Thrifty ——————— Bougie

Saver ——————— Spender

Punctual ——————— Tardy

Finance is Not My Fave ——————— Interested in Finance

No Financial Goals Yet ——————— I've Set Some Goals

Need-Based Aid ——————— Merit-Based Aid

HAVE YOU HAD A TALK
ABOUT FINANCES WITH
YOUR PARENT(S), GUARDIAN(S),
OR HIGH SCHOOL COUNSELOR?

 HOW DID IT GO?

 HOW DO YOU EXPECT IT WILL GO?

CIRCLE THE TYPES OF JOBS YOU'D LIKE TO TRY IN COLLEGE

Barista

Teaching Assistant (TA)

Social Media Intern

Research Assistant

Resident Advisor (RA)

Band Conductor

Library Attendant

Tour Guide

Editor

Tutor

Office Assistant

Athletic Trainer

Nanny

Fitness Instructor

Student Center Manager

Receptionist

Restaurant Server

Choreographer

Camp Counselor

Dog Walker

Production Assistant

Summer Intern

Marketing Intern

Mentor to Kids

• • •

WHAT STRENGTHS WILL YOU BRING TO A JOB?

_____

_____

_____

_____

_____

_____

_____

_____

_____

_____

_____

_____

_____

_____

_____

_____

_____

_____

What would your ideal boss/manager be like?

How do you feel today?

Circle at least one

tell me more!

Building College Connections

* When applying to schools, one of the most complicated pieces has nothing to do with a student's essays or college applications. Filling out financial aid forms can be complex, and students typically won't be able to do this on their own.

* You'll need to provide information about how much money your family members earn, how many people live in your home, and your family's savings accounts among other things. The process can feel quite overwhelming.

* The financial aid forms you fill out will determine your family's "expected contribution." Keep in mind that a family's willingness to pay is not the same as their ability to pay. That's why it is so important to have these conversations early on.

* This may be the first time you are thinking or talking about finances with others. There's no need to worry! If it's a new topic, start small. Simply engaging in this conversation and asking your family about paying for college is a good first step.

* Here are a few things to be aware of:

  → The financial aid application timeline occurs alongside the college application process.

  → Every school in the country is required to have a cost calculator on their financial aid website. Filling this out will provide an estimate of what it might cost you to attend. You can also compare different schools to each other.

→ The "sticker price" of a school is not necessarily what a family will be asked to pay. Some schools that initially appear quite expensive might offer grants or scholarships, which can make them affordable.

→ Most schools will have application fee waivers for students from low-income households. Just ask!

* If you're confused, don't be afraid to reach out to a financial aid officer with your questions. You can always do this before you apply. Financial aid officers are real people who want to help.

Making It Concrete

Tips for discussing finances and applying for aid

* **Timing is everything**. Having a conversation about finances isn't something you should do while running out the door or when everyone might be distracted. Make sure you set aside time for a (potentially) long and focused discussion.

* **Keep your emotions in check**. A school on your list, which might be a good fit academically and socially, might not work for your family financially. Don't worry! There will be other schools that offer similar opportunities and fit your family's financial situation.

* **Practice advocating for yourself**. Finances are situational, and the schools you apply to should be willing to take your specific circumstances into consideration. This may require reaching out to colleges directly. If you don't ask, then you won't know.

* **Apply for outside scholarships**. There are many non-profit organizations, foundations, and corporations that offer scholarships to help students pay for college. Ask people you know (your counselor, friends, family, neighbors, community members, etc.) if they're aware of any sources of funding that can help reduce costs.

* **Don't wait until the last minute**. Some financial aid is awarded based on the date you submit the forms. Make sure to keep track of when these forms become available as well as the deadlines for submitting. It can also take a while to gather information and fill out the documents. Leave yourself enough time to complete the financial aid process.

DAY 28

Environment

Colleges aren't soul mates;
there's more than one for everyone

GOALS

RECOGNIZE WHAT YOU'RE LOOKING FOR IN A COLLEGE EXPERIENCE; IDENTIFY YOUR DEAL BREAKERS

THIS OR THAT
circle one in each pair

Lecture	or	Discussion
Reading	or	Experimenting
Warm All Year	or	Four Seasons
Experiential	or	Theoretical
Essay	or	Problem Set
Game Day	or	Poetry Slam
Walking	or	Driving
Close to Home	or	Far from Home
Art Shows	or	Intramurals
Lab	or	Library
Internship	or	Co-Op
Roommate	or	Suite Style
Sports	or	Arts
City Vibes	or	One with Nature

What will make college feel like a home?

SHARE SOME "MUST HAVES" IN YOUR COLLEGE EXPERIENCE

Which is most important to you right now?

Describe or sketch your ideal
college environment

MINDFULNESS MOMENT:

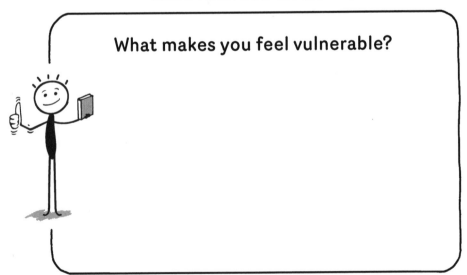

What makes you feel vulnerable?

Building College Connections

* One of the most common sayings in the college search is "find your fit."

* As you build your college list and decide where to apply, you may or may not feel like you've found your "dream school." In reality, there isn't just one perfect college for each student. Every applicant can be amazing, successful, and happy at a variety of schools.

* Most importantly, you should identify the type of institution that is a good fit for **you** and apply to a range of options that meet your needs.

* Remember: "fit" refers to **your** specific <u>academic</u> success, <u>social</u> experience, and <u>financial</u> situation. It means something different to each and every applicant.

* A college's environment can impact your whole college experience. It will shape the campus culture and determine the opportunities available outside of the classroom. A school's physical environment may also attract a certain type of student or professor.

* Reflect on what you're looking for as well as what the college has to offer. Ideally, there will be many similarities and overlaps between what you want and what the college has.

* As you write your college essays, try to be honest and authentic about the environment you are seeking. When a school is a good fit, the essay writing process may feel a bit easier.

Making It Concrete ✦

Envisioning the environment

* Finding your fit means identifying a school that feels like home. As you'll recall from Day 3, a home is more than just a physical location. Environment works the same way.

* Consider these questions as you think about where you want to attend college:

  → Can you picture yourself in a rural, urban, or suburban setting?

  → Is a small, medium, or large campus the right place for you?

  → How do you hope to spend your weekends? For example:

    → Are you someone who wants to have access to art or cultural experiences such as exploring museums or attending live music events?

    → Is it important to be near outdoor activities? If so, would you rather hike a trail, climb a mountain, or go to the beach?

Sample Search

* Rose lives an hour away from a large city. She enjoys participating in many different activities including softball, art classes, cheerleading, and working at a clothing store. However, none of these are "must haves" for Rose's future college experience. Additionally, she hasn't yet chosen a specific academic area or career path to pursue.

* When her older sister left for college, Rose visited the small suburban school. It was a great fit for her sibling, but Rose struggled to picture herself there.

* As she thinks about the type of environment where she feels most comfortable, Rose quickly realizes that an urban setting is what she is looking for.

* Every time she goes downtown, Rose falls in love with the environment. She gets excited to try new restaurants, attend major league baseball games, and walk around the city's distinct neighborhoods.

* Rose conducts a national college search and filters for schools with an urban location. She double checks that they have a professional baseball team and art museums nearby. She finds many great options around the country!

DAY 29

Essays

Trust your intuition
and live with authenticity

GOALS

REVIEW YOUR
PREVIOUS ENTRIES;
OUTLINE SOME POTENTIAL
COLLEGE ESSAY TOPICS

Choose a section
of this journal you'd
like to share with
someone you trust

Which chapter did you choose?

SHARE
IT!

What did they say?

How do you feel?

Describe something you are
thankful for. How has it
impacted or shaped you?

CHOOSE THREE QUESTIONS FROM THIS JOURNAL YOU COULD EXPAND ON

1. _____

2. _____

3. _____

Circle the one you're most excited about

1.   2.   3.

Use this blank space to write a more detailed response

MORE
BLANK
SPACE!

(speech bubble:) YOU'VE GOT THIS!

MINDFULNESS MOMENT:

Share something you've learned about yourself this month

Building College Connections

Tips for writing the college essay

* **Take time to edit, spell-check, and proofread**. Make sure your application materials are error-free and consistent.

* **Every word should be yours**. During the editing process, other people can and should make suggestions. However, all content that is added should be written by you in your own voice.

* **Overwriting is overrated**. Don't worry about finding big, fancy words. You can look smart without the thesaurus! Remember that the people reading your application are not doing so with a dictionary in hand.

* **Tone is everything**. Try to keep the essay positive even if the topic is heavy. Along those lines, you should only write what you are comfortable sharing.

* **Context is key**. Admissions officers care about your background, identity, and context. They look to see what opportunities were available to you in your specific high school, neighborhood, state, and region. Feel free to include information about this if it's relevant.

* **Focus on you**. Even if other people or places are present in your essay, make sure you remain the main subject of the story. The essay should also be from your point of view.

* **Show, don't tell**. Take the reader on the journey by setting the scene and demonstrating the things you describe. Make sure to bring the essay to the present quickly.

* **Don't try to be unique**. Essay topics don't have to be ground-breaking to be great. Ultimately your essay should be authentic and communicate your core values. Some of the best written essays start with basic or everyday topics.

* **Be yourself**. Your identity, personality, and college search will differ from those around you. That's a good thing.

* **Don't worry too much about choosing a topic**. Any of the chapters in the *College Essay Journal* can be themes for your personal statement.

Making It Concrete

Key takeaways

* Apply to schools that fit your academic, social, and financial needs.

* Focus on finding the community where you will thrive.

* Remain open to exploring new opportunities as they come along.

* Pursue majors, activities, and curiosities that bring you happiness.

* Seek out support when you need it.

* Don't take yourself or this process too seriously.

* Remember to laugh and set aside time for you.

Stay mindful!

* Filling out your college applications is a big accomplishment.

* Take time to appreciate the process and be proud of all you've achieved so far.

* Mindfulness techniques can help you stay in the present moment, remain positive, and celebrate how far you have come.

DAY 30

Reflections

Make decisions
out of courage and not fear

GOALS

ACKNOWLEDGE ALL
THE AMAZING WORK
YOU'VE ACCOMPLISHED
OVER THE LAST 30 DAYS!

IT'S THE LAST DAY! HOW DO YOU FEEL?

Circle at least one

> tell me more!

Which section(s) did you enjoy the most? ←-----

GO BACK THROUGH THE JOURNAL

Which section(s) challenged you the most?

 GIVE YOURSELF A COMPLIMENT!
YOU MADE IT TO THE END!

What three values or traits do you want to demonstrate in your college essays?

What are you most excited to share about yourself?

LIST SOME PEOPLE WHO HAVE HELPED YOU ALONG THE WAY

_____

_____

_____

_____

_____

_____

Who can you ask for support going forward?

_____

What did you gain from this journal?

(besides college essay content)

FINAL MINDFULNESS MOMENT:

There is no secret to college essays.

You've had the answers

in your mind the entire time.

Now they also exist in

your *College Essay Journal.*

Finding Your Footing

* When you're ready, answer the prompt on the following page.

* This can be in the form of a full essay, a few paragraphs, or a bullet-point list. Write what comes to you!

* **Tip**: you may want to use the "storyline format" from previous sections (theme, takeaway, and topics).

Reflect on a time when you grew or
changed (for the better) in some way. Tell the story
and share the new perspective you gained.

YOU'RE DOING GREAT!

YOU DID IT!

Acknowledgments

There are so many people and moments that have helped us get here.

To begin, this journal and our identities are inspired by the family, friends, mentors, teachers, coworkers, and classmates who've appeared in our personal timelines. Our perspective is shaped and influenced by our relationships, homes, academic pursuits, communities, activities, travel, intellectual curiosities, environments, and life experiences.

With this book, we hope to have a small impact on the journey of students around the world while making the college application and essay writing process a little less stressful. So thank you for putting time and effort into completing the *College Essay Journal*! It may have been challenging at times, but we hope it brought happiness, reflection, and a bit of mindfulness to your life. Also, laughter! Never forget to laugh.

While the future is yet to be written, we are grateful to have each other as well as some wonderful people in our lives. Our friends and family support us emotionally (and sometimes financially), put up with our ridiculous personalities, and value the qualities we bring to the oversized dinner table. We love you all so much.

About
the Authors

CORINNE SMITH AND ANN MERRELL met in the fall of 2014 on their first day of graduate school at Northwestern University. The rest is history! It's been a best friendship filled with deep dish pizza, funny movies, recreational sports leagues, memorable trips, and an immense love of education.

CORINNE works as an undergraduate admissions officer at Yale University. During her time working in the Yale and Northwestern admissions offices, she has read thousands of applications and served as a voting member on both domestic and international admissions committees. She also volunteers as an academic advisor to first- and second-year college students. Corinne is currently pursuing her doctorate in Diversity and Equity in Education through the University of Illinois Urbana-Champaign.

ANN manages a college readiness program in Chicago. Each year she supports 150+ students from primarily first-generation and low-income backgrounds as they make their way through the college application process. In this role, Ann advises students as they develop a college list, write their college essays, and apply for scholarships and financial aid. She also oversees programming focused on leadership development, civic engagement, college advising, academic inquiry, and cultural exploration.

Corinne and Ann are thrilled to share their knowledge and expertise through the *College Essay Journal*!

Make sure to check out **www.collegeessayjournal.com**
for more college application resources.

Made in the USA
Columbia, SC
08 June 2022

61488728R00146